Sutton Hoo

Paul Dowswell

Contents

The Death of a King

The king was dead, and for the people of Anglo-Saxon East Anglia, it was a time of great sadness and anxiety. With his passing the whole of the kingdom lay open to uncertainty...

Today was the day of his burial. A large, sea-going ship had been hauled up the hill from the Deben River, and laid in a freshly dug pit in the burial ground of Sutton Hoo, near Ipswich in Suffolk. In the centre of the hull, a wooden chamber had been prepared for the king's body, and surrounding the body was an amazing collection of royal possessions. Each one had been chosen with great care, for each had a special significance. There were spears, an axe, a sword and a mighty shield, for the King was a great warrior. There was a sceptre and an iron standard – the symbols of his power. There were ivory drinking horns, wooden ale tubs and a great bronze cauldron – reminders of a time when the dead man had thrown banquets for his lieutenants and allies.

Most impressive of all was a magnificent jewelled silver battle helmet. It was intricate and beautiful, and designed to instil fear and wonder in any who saw the warrior who wore it. Overlooking the mourners filing past the ship to bid farewell to their departed leader, was the queen.

It was she who had taken command of this royal burial, and had chosen the array of fabulous treasures that accompanied her husband in his grave. Also there among the treasure were poignant reminders of their everyday life together – his washbowl, his shoes and even a cap made from otter-fur.

Then, when their ceremonies were completed, men began to cover the ship with earth, until a great mound stood out from the high, flat ground. The mound was both a memorial to the king, and also a monument to his people's hopes for the future. The mound would be visible for miles around – a symbol of the greatness of the king and the power of his dynasty. The king would rest amongst his kinsmen. For Sutton Hoo was a royal burial site and other dignitaries lay beneath its ceremonial mounds.

As the dusk enveloped the windswept hill top, the mourners drifted away to find comfort and solace by their firesides. The great mound was left alone to the vast, darkening sky. In time,

the dreams of those who buried their king at Sutton Hoo would turn to dust.

Other kings and cultures would come to take or change their lives. In all that time, as dynasties rose and fell, seasons and generations came and went, the king lay there undisturbed for over a thousand years. Until 1939…

Who were the Anglo-Saxons?

The people who buried their king at Sutton Hoo have been judged unfairly by history. They come from an era known as the Dark Ages, which stretched from the fifth to the tenth centuries AD.

Above:
The ruins of
Housesteads Fort.
The fort was sited
on Hadrian's Wall
and housed many
soldiers.

We call this era the Dark Ages because few written records were made to tell us about what life was like during this time.

For the first 400 years of the first millennium, Britain was part of the Roman Empire. But when the empire began to weaken, the Romans withdrew their armies in AD410 to defend their home territory. Without them, their magnificent buildings and houses, bathhouses and amphitheatres, aqueducts and roads, all fell to ruin. The remaining Britons came under attack from tribes in the north of the island, known as the Picts. Even the mighty Roman army had only been able to keep them at bay rather than conquer them. In desperation, the Britons called on Saxon mercenaries to help protect them.

Roman Life

The Romans built towns and cities in Britain. These towns were centres for trading and tax collection. Trade relied upon money to prosper. As the Romans retreated to defend other parts of their empire, new coins stopped arriving in Britain Without coinage taxes weren't collected and trade suffered. As a result the Romans' towns and cities fell into disrepair as they could not be maintained without the wealth generated by commerce.

This page:
The impressive remains of a
Roman Villa in
Chedworth,
Gloucestershire

Where did they come from?

The Saxons were a mixed blessing. They kept back the invading tribes, but when the Britons could no longer pay them, they turned on their hosts and ravaged the countryside.

Even worse, they sent back reports to their kin in Europe, telling of rich, poorly defended land, ripe for settlement.

Saxons, Angles and Jutes from an area that is now Denmark, The Netherlands and Germany, poured over the North Sea and into Britain. Many Britons were slaughtered or fled to the outer edges of their island – Scotland, Wales and Cornwall – where their descendants live to this day. However, many other Britons adapted to the invaders' way of life, culture and laws – eventually becoming 'Anglo-Saxons'.

The Anglo-Saxons have been depicted as hooligans who couldn't read or write, keen on fighting and drinking, with little time for the finer things in life. The burial ground at Sutton Hoo shows this to be untrue.

The Saxons would control England for the next 600 years. But their era came to an end when the Duke of Normandy, William the Conqueror, killed the last Anglo-Saxon king, Harold II, at the Battle of Hastings in 1066. During the time of the Anglo-Saxons, England first began to resemble the country we know today.

A Germanic language replaced the Celtic or Latin spoken in Roman Britain, and evolved into English, the language we now speak. As powerful families and military leaders took control of particular areas, the country took on many of the regions and counties it still has. Gradually, small kingdoms were forged into one central power. The Anglo-Saxon era laid down roots that Britain, particularly England, was to build on for the next 1,500 years.

Buried treasure

The burial ground at Sutton Hoo was never a secret site.

Until Christianity came to East Anglia in the seventh century, it was a respected sacred spot. When the new religion took hold it became a sinister place. So much so that executions were held there. Aside from violent death, victims suffered the double punishment of being buried in pagan, or non-Christian, ground – further torment for their corrupted souls.

For a thousand years the site was left undisturbed. It was widely believed that dragons guarded the burial mounds, and who would want to risk an encounter with a fire-breathing monster for the sake of a few trinkets?

By the sixteenth century, belief in dragons had faded. Royal permission was gained to investigate the graves, and their contents were carried off and lost to history. Most were probably melted down to fashion other treasures and jewels more suited to the taste of the people who found them.

In the mound of the mighty king, grave robbers dug very close to the ship's burial chamber. As a fierce wind blew in from the coast, they huddled in their freshly made pit, lit a fire and passed around a flagon of wine. Then the pit began to collapse around them and they hurriedly scrambled out. We know this, because traces of a fire, and the pottery wine bottle,

were later discovered. In 1860 the site was investigated again. But these Victorians found little to interest them save many iron ship rivets. These were passed on to a local blacksmith to melt down to make horseshoes.

In the late 1930s the investigation of Sutton Hoo began in earnest. The owner of the nearby mansion house, Edith Pretty, had become interested in archaeology during a holiday in Egypt. In 1938 she employed a local archaeologist named Basil Brown to dig up mounds on the outer edge of her estate. Brown was helped by Guy Maynard, curator of the Ipswich Corporation Museum.

Brown and Maynard opened three of the mounds. All of the mounds had been looted by robbers some time before the excavation. However, the archaeologists found evidence that two of the mounds contained cremated burials and the third held traces of a buried boat. They also found ornaments of glass and metal and the remains of iron weapons. In 1939, they began to dig up the biggest mound and unearthed the outline of a large ship. Charles Philips of Cambridge University was called in to help with further excavations.

What they had discovered was one of the most exciting and important archaeological finds from the Dark Ages, and of the Anglo-Saxons who had ruled over East Anglia during this mysterious period.

Opposite page:
This vessel is a reconstruction of a typical Saxon ship.

This page:
Top:
Edith Pretty

Bottom:
Basil Brown

Further finds

After the war a British Museum team re-investigated the ship burial and its surroundings. The discovered artefacts were cleaned, analysed, preserved and sometimes even reconstructed.

By the 1980s, more graves had been found. Many were of important individuals who had been cremated and their remains placed in metal urns. Those buried in such graves almost certainly belonged to the same family as the king whose grave had been discovered in 1939. Placed close to them were items to indicate their high standing among their people. These items tell us much about their lives and culture. They were warriors who enjoyed hunting and feasting. One is even buried with his beloved horse.

In the 1980s, a further study of the site was carried out under archaeologist Martin Carver. Many of the discoveries on this dig were more sinister, although no less intriguing. The bodies in the graves unearthed had been executed. These date from a later period than the previously discovered graves, when Christianity had replaced the Anglo-Saxon's pagan beliefs. The dead, who had been strangled, hanged or beheaded, were thrown willy-nilly into shallow pits. Their sprawling postures and lack of grave goods make a poignant and brutal contrast with the care and respect shown to Sutton Hoo's more esteemed residents (see page 28).

Neighbouring Dynasties

In autumn 2003 archaeologists made a remarkable discovery in Prittlewell, Essex. An exploration unearthed the grave of what is believed to be a seventh-century Anglo-Saxon king. Interestingly, this burial took place not long after the death of the great king at Sutton Hoo.

The grave itself was formed of a chamber containing grave goods under a mound, indicating that the burial was of someone of very high status. Like Sutton Hoo this grave contained symbols of wealth and kingship; a great sword, drinking horns and a beautiful gold belt buckle. It also contained gold foil crosses indicating that whoever was buried here, was, at least outwardly, of Christian faith.

No trace of a body was found in the grave. However, archaeologists believe that the burial is most likely to be that of a king of the East Saxons whose kingdom covered Essex, Middlesex and included Lundenwic, a trading centre that would eventually grow into one of the world's greatest cities – London.

SUTTON HOO 1991 INT 48
F 318   STAGE 9

Top:
Companions
through life and
death, the
warrior and his
horse
(see page 40).

The Sutton Hoo mystery

So revealing and important were the findings at Sutton Hoo, it has been described as "page one of English history".

But, two unsolved mysteries surround the ship and its treasures. Firstly, whose grave is it? Secondly, is there actually a body there at all?

Archaeologists believe that the grave is most likely to be that of the Anglo-Saxon king **Rædwald** (pronounced Redwald). Saxon legends tell us that the king died around AD625. Evidence from the ship itself suggests that it was buried at about this time. (Coins found in the grave, for example, were from no later than this date.) We cannot be certain as the Saxons did not formally record their history. However, Rædwald was certainly important enough to be afforded an impressive burial.

But nothing in the grave, such as an engraved ring or an inscribed stone, tells us about who might have been buried there. That's not to say there never was any evidence. But anything organic – that is, made of once-living material such as wood, or wool – has rotted away.

The body inside the grave has also rotted away, so much so that some archaeologists think the ship might be a cenotaph – a memorial with no one in it – rather than a grave. But most people who have investigated the site think there was a body. Decaying bodies leave large traces of a chemical known as phosphate.

Modern forensic techniques, used by the police to investigate corpses, have detected such traces on items found in the grave.

What almost certainly happened to the body is this: as Rædwald lay in his burial chamber, water seeped in. Soil at Sutton Hoo is very acidic, so the water would pick this up. Gradually, water filled the chamber, covering the body in an acid-rich pool. Over time, the body, bones and all, were dissolved away. When the acid water also ate through the hull of the boat, the whole mixture ran out, dispersing whatever was left of the king into the soil beneath. The weight of earth above the chamber also caused it to collapse, and Rædwald's carefully created burial space was engulfed with soil.

Archaeologists have reconstructed items made of organic material. For example, the wooden gaming board and beaver-skin bag.

East Anglia and the Anglo-Saxons

Anglo-Saxons first began to arrive in what was to become East Anglia in around AD400.

Many were hired as mercenaries, for their fighting prowess was well known. However, relations between natives and newcomers soon broke down, not least because when the Romans departed, a great influx of Saxons from Europe arrived. The newcomers had no intention of blending in with the locals. They set up their own settlements away from the fading splendour of the Roman towns.

At first there was a clear division between the Saxons. Two separate clans established

themselves in the counties that still bear their names – the South Folk (Suffolk) and the North Folk (Norfolk). But these two rivals were united by a family known as the Wuffingas (meaning Wolf's People). Rædwald was a Wuffinga, perhaps the greatest one of all. Gradually, the Saxons began to build towns such as Ipswich, in East Anglia. It was known as Gipeswic, 'wic' being a Germanic word for a trading centre.

By AD600, the time of Rædwald's reign, the kingdom of East Anglia was still defiantly pagan, although many of its neighbours were Christian kingdoms, both to the south, in Kent, and over the North Sea, in continental Europe. Rædwald and his subjects must have felt isolated and fearful that their traditions and freedom were under threat from this new religion and the nations who were uniting under its wing.

Noble, churl or slave

Under the Wuffingas, a society with three distinct classes developed. There were the nobles, the land-owning aristocracy. Beneath them were the churls, small farmers and peasants. At the bottom of the social heap were slaves. Some were prisoners captured in wars. Some were criminals. Some were desperately poor, and had sold themselves to wealthy men in exchange for food to keep them from starving. These social divisions were common throughout all the Anglo-Saxon kingdoms of England.

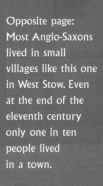

Opposite page: Most Anglo-Saxons lived in small villages like this one in West Stow. Even at the end of the eleventh century only one in ten people lived in a town.

Rædwald and Anglo-Saxon society

Rædwald was buried with several symbols of kingship, no doubt meant to indicate his importance to his family and clan.

In the tomb are the emblems of kingly authority – a sceptre and a tall iron standard, his weapons, and items to indicate his role as a great host. The grave contained ivory drinking horns, a lyre (a type of harp) and finger bowls. It was a king's job to entertain his commanders at banquets, where great matters of state were discussed, and arguments resolved over splendid feasts and gallons of wine or beer.

It would be wrong to say these 'prove' for sure that he was a king. During this time, many local rulers put on the airs of royalty, without the substance and power to back it up. But Rædwald was almost certainly different. During his reign all of the separate Anglo-Saxon kingdoms of England came under his influence, if not direct control.

Aside from items buried in his tomb, what we know about Rædwald comes from an account written a hundred years after his death, by a monk named Bede (see page 27). Bede says that Rædwald had shown an interest in Christianity but had returned to his pagan beliefs. He tried to keep a foot in both camps. His temple, noted Bede, contained altars to both Christianity and pagan gods.

The area around Sutton Hoo has strong associations with kingship through its place names. Near to the burial ground are Ufford (meaning Wuffa or Wuffinga's place) and Kingston (meaning the King's town). These names make it more likely that this was the royal centre of East Anglia and that the bodies buried at Sutton Hoo, especially in the more elaborate graves, are members of an Anglo-Saxon royal family.

Rædwald's queen

Recorded history has left us very little about mighty King Rædwald, so it's not surprising that we know even less about his queen, not even her name.

Through Bede we know that Rædwald's queen was a woman of great moral character. When Edwin, a Northumbrian prince, was hiding from his enemy Aethelfrith, King of

Left:
This coin features Queen Cynethryth, wife of King Offa of Mercia. It is a rare example of a queen featuring on a coin.

Northumbria, he sought refuge in Rædwald's court. Aethelfrith offered Rædwald a large sum of money to kill or hand over Edwin. Rædwald was tempted by this offer, but his queen persuaded him not to do this. Bede writes that she advised him: "It is not fitting for a king to sell his friends for gold: much less, for love of money, to sacrifice his honour, which is more precious than any ornament."

Not everything Bede has to say about Rædwald's queen is so flattering. Bede blames her for persuading him to turn his back on Christianity, as she was determined to resist this new religion and remain a worshipper of the pagan gods. It may have been her role as his wife to organise his burial. It was under her influence that his grave is both pagan and Christian.

Women in Anglo-Saxon England

Women in Anglo-Saxon times had fewer rights than today, but some still rose to positions of importance. The wife of a king or an Abbess (a women in charge of a convent of nuns), for example, would have considerable power and influence. Bede tells us that Rædwald's queen had a great deal of influence in his kingdom. Women could own land, and inherit from their fathers or husbands. Marriages, especially of aristocratic women, were usually arranged between families. But a woman had the right to refuse a husband she did not want, and she could leave him if the marriage turned out badly.

Opposite page:
Top:
Anglo-Saxons took great care of their appearance. They kept their long hair and beards tidy with combs like this one.

This page:
Anglo-Saxon women were skilled weavers (see page 36).

Warfare and weaponry

If a king was not a warrior, he was nothing.

The Anglo-Saxon era was a violent one. Anglo-Saxons left very few written accounts of life as they would have known it. However, they did leave some poems, such as *Beowulf*, and the *Battle of Brunanburh*, which give vivid descriptions of the terror of hand to hand fighting. *Beowulf,* for example, speaks of "sweeping slaughter" where "battle death bore off each of the men". This was an age before cannons and gunpowder. When men met their death in war, it was to be bludgeoned, impaled or mutilated by axe, spear or sword.

A king held power by virtue of his leadership, often in battle. His enemies were many, especially in the early years of the era. There were rivals within his dynasty, other local leaders and kingdoms, and foreign invaders. We do not know if Rædwald met a violent death, but if he died of old age, he was probably the exception rather than the rule.

The splendid ornamentation and craftsmanship of his weapons tell us that they were of great importance. Buried with him are a magnificent helmet, and a beautifully crafted sword and shield. Spears and a battle axe were also placed in the grave.

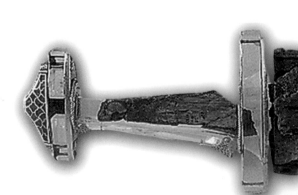

Weapon ownership was commonplace among free Anglo-Saxon men, although slaves would not have carried weapons. Spears were often placed in graves, but swords are rarely found. It took time to make such carefully forged weapons, and the precious iron they were made from made them almost too valuable to squander in burial. The fact that Rædwald's family thought it fitting to bury him with such magnificent weapons tells us a great deal about his wealth and power.

Spears, swords, shields and axes were all essential items for a warrior king.

Rædwald's ship

The ship Rædwald was buried in tells us that the Anglo-Saxons were great boat builders.

Although the wooden vessel has rotted away in the acid soil, we still have a good idea of how it was built, because the planks and rivets of its hull left a clear imprint in the sand. The construction is solid, and ingeniously put together. Recently, a replica boat of half the original size was built to the same design, and it sailed beautifully (see page 11). Rædwald's ship was a working vessel

We know this because archaeologists discovered that the hull had been repaired. It's most likely that the ship was buried because it was either Rædwald's or at least closely associated with him. Although it is highly likely, we do not know for certain whether the boat had a sail, because the central section had been rebuilt to make the burial chamber. There were also spaces for oarsmen –

probably 28 in all, 14 on either side, for when the wind dropped, and human muscle power was needed to move the boat instead. The boat was a sea-going vessel, which could have crossed the North Sea or sailed around the British coast. It could have been used for a great many purposes. Anglo-Saxon boats carried royal passengers and their court and guards, and were also used to carry crops and cattle,

trading goods, pilgrims and raiders. It was often quicker and easier to transport goods and people by sea rather than overland. Overland travel was made difficult and dangerous by the lack of good roads and journeys through neighbouring and potentially hostile kingdoms. Some of the treasures in Rædwald's grave came from as far away as the eastern Mediterranean.

Religion and the Anglo-Saxons

Anglo-Saxon religion was changing during the time of Rædwald's rule.

In AD597 St Augustine arrived in Kent from Rome and began to convert the Anglo-Saxons to Christianity. Britain had been a Christian region before, during the time of the Romans, but the arrival of the Anglo-Saxons had extinguished or driven this religion underground.

The Anglo-Saxons believed in pagan gods, the most important of which was Nerthus the earth mother, who looked after both people and animals. Many of their gods had much in

common with those worshipped by their Northern European ancestors. There was Woden, the god of the sun and wisdom, Thor, the god of thunder, and Freya the goddess of love. All of these gods were still worshipped by Scandinavian Vikings four centuries after Rædwald's death.

The Kentish King Aethelbert was the first Anglo-Saxon king to convert to Christianity. We know that Rædwald visited Kent and returned to East Anglia as a Christian convert. But shortly after his return he reverted to his old gods, and was buried as a pagan.

Among the treasures in Rædwald's grave, there are items of Christian significance, such as silver bowls and spoons which have 'Saulos' and 'Paulos' written on them (see below, left). This is almost certainly a reference to St Paul, the Christian martyr. These valuable items

might have been a gift to Rædwald from Aethelbert, when he converted to Christianity. But they could also be plunder, or traded goods. Rædwald might have treasured them for their beauty and value rather than their religious significance – we shall never know.

Christianity brought great changes to the Anglo-Saxon way of life. Written records became more commonplace (although most people still couldn't read or write), and learning and study became respectable pursuits. In the century after Rædwald died, nearly 200 monasteries were founded in England. In these religious centres, beautiful hand-written books were produced. The most famous of these are the Lindisfarne Gospels. The illustrations in them were so ornate and magnificent that people who saw them thought they had been made by angels.

The Venerable Bede

Bede, who lived from AD 673–735, wrote a great account of Anglo-Saxon times called *The Ecclesiastical History of the English People*. It is the main source of information about life in England during this period. Bede is such an important figure to the Christian Church and to historians that he is often called the Venerable Bede, venerable meaning greatly respected.

Opposite page:
Top:
The design and beauty of the Lindisfarne Gospels is as striking today as over a thousand years ago.

The Killing Place

Soon after Rædwald's death, Christianity took root in East Anglia.

The burial ground of a pagan king became a sinister spot, touched by evil. This is why Sutton Hoo was used as a killing place – *cwealmstow* – to use the Anglo-Saxon word, and a burial ground for victims.

Situated in the eastern side of the burial grounds, it makes a bleak spot. Those beheaded or hanged would have looked out over a vast horizon, as the view east around Sutton Hoo is of a great flat plain. Chilly winds sweep in from the nearby North Sea coast, and witnesses would never know whether those about to die were shaking from fear or cold.

The bodies of those executed at Sutton Hoo lie in crumpled postures – thrown like discarded dolls into shallow graves with a brutal lack of ceremony. Like Rædwald, their remains have gone completely, but the soil around them has formed into the shape of their twisted bodies. They are known as the Sand People, and there

What price a man's life?

In Anglo-Saxon times, a man's life was valued by the social class he came from. If he was killed, his murderer would have to pay his family a set amount in compensation, or face execution. So, those who were executed were usually the poorest members of society. Because the value of money has changed so much over the centuries, it is difficult to understand how much a particular sum is worth today. But to give you some idea, in Anglo-Saxon times one pound could buy you eight oxen. A slave's life was worth one pound, a churl's was ten pounds and a noble's sixty pounds.

are 17 of them, all showing signs of a violent death. In one grave lie the bodies of a decapitated man with two women, also violently killed. What strange, sad story led to their deaths, has been lost in time.

This page: The Sand People are a poignant reminder of Sutton Hoo's change in status from royal burial ground to execution site.

Language, writing and song

Very few of the items in Rædwald's tomb have writing on them.

This is not surprising, as most Anglo-Saxons could not read or write. If they did write, they used runes – symbols with magical meaning quite unlike the alphabet we use today. But the remains of a lyre in the burial chamber hints at the importance of song and music in Rædwald's life. Stories of the deeds of kings or great warriors were remembered in epic poems, which were then performed by a musician known as a bard, at feasts or other special ceremonies. Bards were greatly valued by their communities. They were the television, cinema and newspaper of their day.

Anglo-Saxon poetry is bold – what we'd call "in your face" – but it is also curiously melancholic. The Anglo-Saxons were keenly aware that death was always among them. While they enjoyed their life and families and feasting, they knew that these could be snatched away from them in an instant. Many poems stress the importance of loyalty to a king or community.

Beowulf is the most famous poem from Anglo-Saxon times, and there are scenes similar to Rædwald's funeral in its epic verses (see box). The story, however, originated one or two hundred years before the death of Rædwald,

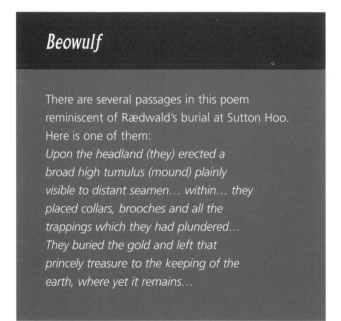

Beowulf

There are several passages in this poem reminiscent of Rædwald's burial at Sutton Hoo. Here is one of them:

Upon the headland (they) erected a broad high tumulus (mound) plainly visible to distant seamen… within… they placed collars, brooches and all the trappings which they had plundered… They buried the gold and left that princely treasure to the keeping of the earth, where yet it remains…

and is set in Southern Scandinavia. The people who buried Rædwald almost certainly knew the poem. Maybe it even influenced the way they carried out the burial.

The Anglo-Saxons spoke a northern Germanic dialect, and when they came to Britain they absorbed a few Celtic and Latin words which we still use today. When the Anglo-Saxon era came to an end with the conquest of the Normans in 1066, the language was strong enough to survive. In fact, the Normans who came to England eventually adopted it to distinguish themselves from their Norman relatives in France.

Left:
Anglo-Saxons used runes as shown on this casket. However, towards the end of their era they began to use the alphabet we recognise today (above right).

Above:
Bards played instruments like this lyre.

Arts and Crafts

When Rædwald's tomb was first unearthed in 1939, archaeologists and historians were astounded by the fine quality of the treasures they found.

Bomb-proof shelter

Rædwald's treasures were discovered only a month or two before the start of the Second World War in September 1939. To protect them from being destroyed by enemy bombers or during a German invasion of England, they were placed in storage in a deep tunnel constructed as part of the London Underground.

The image of Anglo-Saxons as brutish, uncultured people did not fit in with the obvious value they placed on such items and their ability to make them.

There were 19 jewelled pieces among the hoard unearthed in 1939, including an exquisite buckle and purse. Such itemswere made in East Anglia during Rædwald's lifetime. They were almost certainly worn by him as a visible sign of his wealth and power.

Gold, and garnets imported from India, were used with great skill. The red stones, for example, were backed with gold foil to make them sparkle in the light. During Anglo-Saxon times, jewellers were so highly regarded they were thought to have inherited their skills from the gods.

Patterns on the jewellery buried with Rædwald show that the Anglo-Saxons were influenced by both the Celtic culture which had preceded them, and the Northern European culture of their ancestors.

All of these items were discovered in Rædwald's grave. They show the quality and skill of Anglo-Saxon craftsmen.

Feasting and entertainment

Entertaining was one of a king's most important responsibilities.

Here, he and his lieutenants could discuss and resolve problems and disputes. Showing hospitality to other powerful leaders was another way of gaining friendship and influence. Rædwald's power was partly built on the goodwill he created with such feasting and entertainment.

At such events, the loyalty and courage of a king's lieutenants would be rewarded by public displays of gifts and praise. This was important in a society where money as we know it today had no meaning. Gold was valued by its weight.

The importance of feasting to the Anglo-Saxons is plain in the number of items related to eating and drinking found in Rædwald's ship. There are drinking horns, ten silver bowls, a large cauldron, silver spoons, and tubs and buckets.

All of these items are beautifully made, to impress those around him with his power and wealth.

The drinking horns are exquisitely made from the hollowed-out horns of a large bull. The idea of the horn was that it could not be put down without spilling the liquid inside. This encouraged the guests to pass the horn around and share the drink.

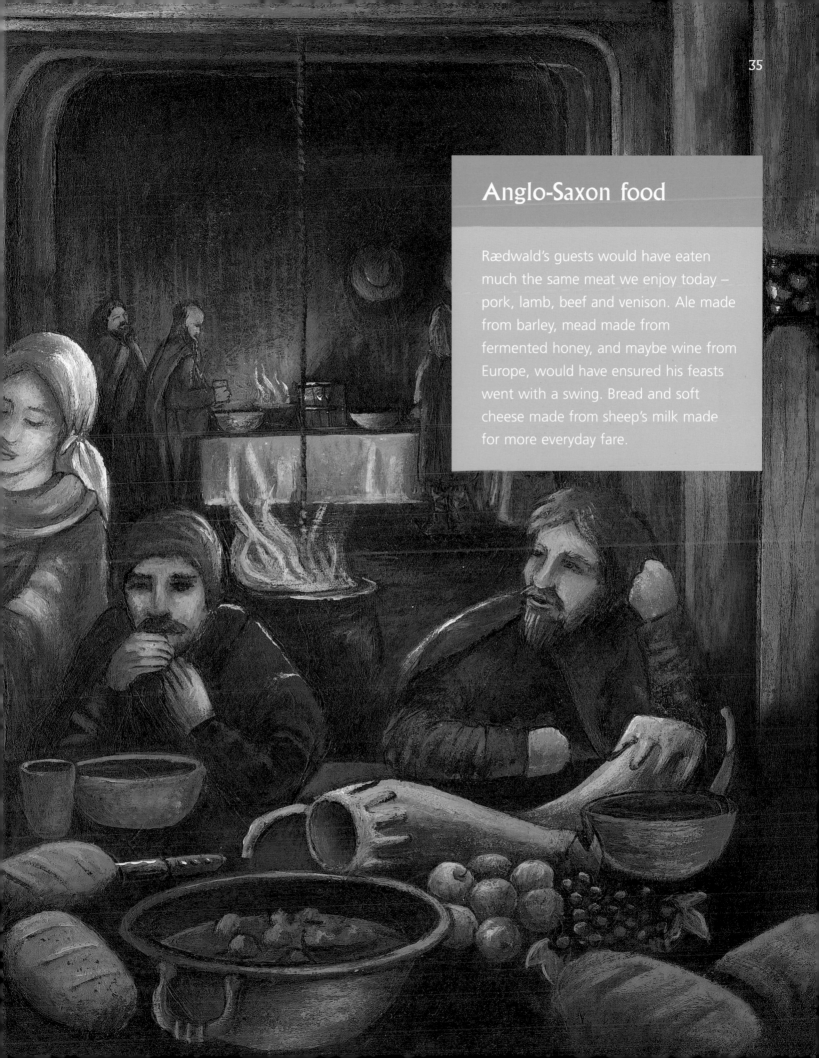

Anglo-Saxon food

Rædwald's guests would have eaten much the same meat we enjoy today – pork, lamb, beef and venison. Ale made from barley, mead made from fermented honey, and maybe wine from Europe, would have ensured his feasts went with a swing. Bread and soft cheese made from sheep's milk made for more everyday fare.

Anglo-Saxon clothing and textiles

Almost everything in Rædwald's ship that was organic – that is, made from living material – was eaten away by the acid soil of Sutton Hoo. Only fragments of clothing and cloth remain, usually those that were used to wrap metal objects.

From these tiny remains, we can piece together some understanding of what sort of clothes the Anglo-Saxons wore. They used animals skins, as we do today, to make leather garments, and also wool (see page 20).

Generally poor people wore clothes made of wool. Richer people had wool clothes too, but also wore clothes made of linen. Linen was more expensive and came from a plant called flax.

The style of the clothes, if not the fabric, was much the same for rich and poor. Men wore tunics, cloaks and trousers. Women wore long dresses. The Anglo-Saxons did not have buttons, so buckles and brooches were used to hold them in place. They would also have had laces or fabric ties to keep them closed. The style of such ornaments varied greatly, depending on the wealth of the wearer. Rich people would wear buckles and brooches made of gold and decorated with jewels.

There were several kinds of fabric found in Rædwald's tomb. The lyre was kept in a beaver-skin bag, for example, and there are remains of cloaks, wall hangings, blankets, tunics, even an otter-fur cap. Some of the textiles may have come from as far as Italy and Syria, showing that these goods were traded and transported hundreds or thousands of miles from their place of origin.

To Dye for

Today, we mainly use dyes made from chemicals. The Anglo-Saxons used natural dyes made from plants, which produced bright, even gaudy, colours. Here are some of them:

Yellow – from onion
Mauve – from lichens
Orange, red and brown – from madder
Blue – from woad (above)

Anglo-Saxon clothes were simple, practical and brightly coloured.

Animals

The Anglo-Saxons were well aware that tending their animals carefully was essential for food, clothing and succesful farming.

They protected their livestock in winter, hunted wild boars and deer, and kept pets. Cattle, sheep and pigs were a vital part of any farm. The deep connection the Anglo-Saxons felt with their fellow creatures can be seen in the art emblazoned upon their weapons, armour and jewellery. The shield found in Rædwald's burial chamber has a fantastic depiction of an eagle, and dragon figures too. Perhaps by depicting fierce and shrewd animal hunters on their weapons and armour the Anglo-Saxons hoped to emulate their skills.

The graves of several of those cremated at Sutton Hoo show that animals were often buried with humans – there are remains of a horse, deer, cow, sheep and pig among the human ashes in the burial bowls. In one mound there is an entire horse beside his master, who lies in the next grave.

Many of the animals found in Anglo-Saxon art form part of a visual language – pagan symbols whose meaning is now largely lost to us. The pagan warrior god Frey, for example, was associated with the wild boar. An item of jewellery or a weapon with a boar symbol on it was thought to offer protection in battle.

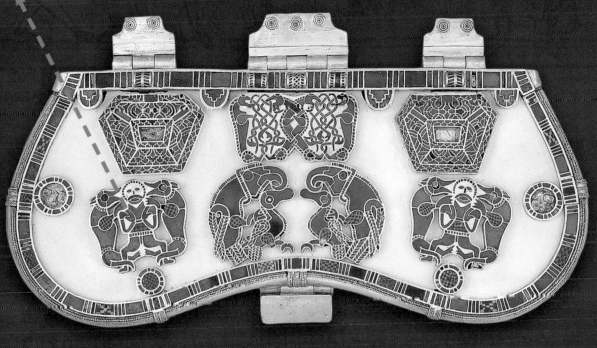

Opposite Page:
This manuscript shows the Anglo-Saxons herding their sheep.

This page:
Top:
One Image found on Rædwald's purse-lid shows a man being attacked by two ferocious wolves.

The warrior and his horse

Considering that Sutton Hoo has been consistently plundered since Elizabethan times, the discovery of a warrior and his horse in 1992 was an unexpected stroke of luck.

When the mound was excavated there were two separate pits. One contained a young man aged about 25. With him were two spears, a shield, a sword, jewellery, and a beautifully decorated harness and bridle made of silver and gold shaped into human and animal figures. These all suggested he was a noble warrior. Also with him was a small knapsack containing lamb chops, and maybe other items such as apples and bread, which have long since vanished into the earth.

In the other pit was a horse – a stallion aged about five or six. It had almost certainly been sacrificed during the burial ceremony to accompany its master. The burial of a sacrificed horse next to a warrior was a common tradition in Germany and Scandinavia during Rædwald's time. The burial at Sutton Hoo offers us further evidence that there were close cultural links between East Anglia's Anglo-Saxons and their Northern European relatives.

Until the twentieth century, warriors on horseback formed an élite in any fighting force. They were drawn from a wealthy social class, which could afford the expense of a horse. A warrior on a horse had speed, manoeuvrability and a high platform from which to fight, giving him a massive advantage over the ordinary foot soldier. The young man buried with his horse at Sutton Hoo presents us with an heroic and romantic image. He sets off for the hereafter with his handsome horse, gleaming gold and silver bridle, and even a picnic to accompany him on his adventure – much as he must have done during his short life on Earth.

Allies and enemies

Although the Anglo-Saxons mainly came from Germany, some historians think that the Wuffingas at Sutton Hoo may have come from Sweden.

Much of their culture finds an echo in the art, religion and poetry of Scandinavia. A helmet, sword and shield similar to ones found at Sutton Hoo have been found at a Scandinavian boat burial at Valsgärde. Similar burial mounds and ship burials are also found at Old Uppsala and Vendel, now in present-day Sweden. The eagle on Rædwald's shield is especially similar to those of Scandinavian design. But it is wise not to draw too many conclusions about the link between the two regions and their inhabitants, because we have so few examples to go on.

Boat burials, for important people, were common in Scandinavia for 400 years. They took place in England for a much briefer period – in fact, the 50 or so years around the time of Rædwald.

There were certainly some connections between the Scandinavians and the Anglo-Saxons of East Anglia. But how far back these connections stretched it is impossible to say. In a boat such as the one in which Rædwald was buried, it would

Anglo-Saxons and Vikings

The Viking era, when the seafaring warriors and traders of Sweden, Norway and Denmark terrorised their more southerly European neighbours, lasted from the eighth to eleventh centuries. For most of the Anglo-Saxon era, the Vikings were yet to be a threat. Only in the late ninth century did they attack England. Then, their impact was tremendous. Half of the country was taken over and named the Danelaw. Northumberland, Mercia and Rædwald's own East Anglia fell under Viking control until the middle of the tenth century.

have taken about two weeks to sail from Sutton Hoo to Sweden. Keeping in touch with relatives would have taken some effort, but is easy enough to imagine. During this era, Europe had a small and highly mobile population. The Wuffingas were part of an international European culture and their way of life was influenced by many different traditions – from the Romans through to the Ancient Britons they usurped.

Opposite page:
Left:
Alfred the Great, King of Wessex, managed to keep the Vikings from controlling the country.

This page:
Left:
Figureheads like this were common to the ships of many peoples in Northern Europe.

Above:
Lindisfarne Abbey was attacked many times by the Vikings.

The end of the Anglo-Saxons

Rædwald and his people brought great changes to this country.

During their time as rulers of England, the Anglo-Saxons saw their religion replaced by Christianity and their language slowly evolve from a Germanic dialect to an English recognisable in thousands of words we use today.

The Anglo-Saxon kingdoms they created – East Anglia, Kent, Northumbria, Wessex, Essex and Mercia – are still recognisable parts of the country. Many English counties, such as Hampshire, Wiltshire, Dorset and Somerset, have their origins in Anglo-Saxon times.

What's in a name?

Many of our villages, towns or cities have their origins in Anglo-Saxon times. You can tell this by their name, which contains an Anglo-Saxon word such as:

ing (people) Spalding
ley (clearing) Dudley
head (hill) Portishead
holt (wood) Northolt
ham (home) Brixham

Old traditions

We keep some old Anglo-Saxon traditions alive without even realising it. Today we celebrate the Christian festival of Easter with chocolate eggs. Rabbits too are a common symbol both on Easter cards and as chocolate gifts. Yet the very name Easter is derived from the Anglo-Saxon's pagan goddess of the dawn and Spring, Eostre. In pagan art, her symbols were the hare and the egg.

The greatest legacy of the Anglo-Saxons is that they united a divided country under one strong central government and common culture. The concept of "England" was one they invented. This mixture of different cultures came to Britain and forged a nation that eventually became a world power, that ruled over one quarter of the world.

Opposite page: The Battle of Hastings in 1066 was closely fought. The Saxon army only weakened after a stray arrow killed King Harold.

This page: After the Normans defeated the Anglo-Saxons at Hastings, they immediately began building fortresses like this castle at Corfe in Dorset to secure their new territory.

Sutton Hoo today

The final resting place of Rædwald, and other members of his East Anglian Anglo-Saxon royal family, is now a splendid National Trust site, which opened in 2002. There is a souvenir shop, and a fascinating exhibition hall, chockfull of Sutton Hoo information, including a carefully recreated depiction of Rædwald's burial chamber. The actual treasures themselves are on display at a special gallery in the British Museum in London, although there are also beautifully recreated replicas at Sutton Hoo.

The burial grounds are roped off, but visitors can peer over to the vast mound where Rædwald was buried, where two wooden poles mark the bow and stern of the ship. The execution spot can also be clearly seen.

There is still much for archaeologists to do at Sutton Hoo and the area surrounding it.

There is an Anglo-Saxon burial ground nearby, containing the remains of "ordinary" people, which, when investigated, will tell us a great deal about how they lived their lives. Altogether there are 17 mounds at Sutton Hoo itself; not all of them have been examined. Archaeologists are confident that future developments in forensics and underground research equipment will enable scientists and historians to investigate further remains far more effectively than they can at present. After all, the people digging things up only get one chance. Despite the care they took, who knows what secrets were lost forever when Basil Brown and Charles Philips conducted their dig in 1939? Undoubtedly we could have learned far more with the forensic and archaeological skills we have today.

Out on the flat plain of Sutton Hoo, a lone pine tree overlooks the remaining mounds. Who knows what secrets lurk beneath its spreading boughs?